BY LOUIS MACNEICE

POEMS

RANDOM HOUSE · NEW YORK

TO THOSE WHOSE HANDS
ARE FRIENDLY

❦ CONTENTS

I. *Poems Published in* 1935

II. *Early Poems*

III. *Later Poems*

I. POEMS PUBLISHED IN 1935

διώκει παῖς ποτανὸν ὄρνιν.

A. I meet you in an evil time.
B.   The evil bells
     Put out of our heads, I think, the thought of every-
          thing else.
A. The jaded calendar revolves,
     Its nuts need oil, carbon chokes the valves,
     The excess sugar of a diabetic culture
     Rotting the nerve of life and literature;
     Therefore when we bring out the old tinsel and frills
     To announce that Christ is born among the barbarous
          hills
     I turn to you whom a morose routine
     Saves from the mad vertigo of being what has been.
B. Analogue of me, you are wrong to turn to me,
     My country will not yield you any sanctuary,
     There is no pinpoint in any of the ordnance maps
     To save you when your towns and town-bred thoughts
          collapse,
     It is better to die *in situ* as I shall,
     One place is as bad as another. Go back where your
          instincts call
     And listen to the crying of the town-cats and the taxis
          again,
     Or wind your gramophone and eavesdrop on great
          men.
A. Jazz-weary of years of drums and Hawaian guitar,
     Pivoting on the parquet I seem to have moved far
     From bombs and mud and gas, have stuttered on my
          feet
     Clinched to the streamlined and butter-smooth trulls
          of the élite,

The lights irritating and gyrating and rotating in
      gauze—
Pomade-dazzle, a slick beauty of gewgaws—
I who was Harlequin in the childhood of the century,
Posed by Picasso beside an endless opaque sea,
Have seen myself sifted and splintered in broken
      facets,
Tentative pencillings, endless liabilities, no assets,
Abstractions scalpelled with a palette-knife
Without reference to this particular life.
And so it has gone on; I have not been allowed to be
Myself in flesh or face, but abstracting and dissecting
      me
They have made of me pure form, a symbol or a
      pastiche,
Stylised profile, anything but soul and flesh:
And that is why I turn this jaded music on
To forswear thought and become an automaton.
B. There are in the country also of whom I am afraid—
Men who put beer into a belly that is dead,
Women in the forties with terrier and setter who
      whistle and swank
Over down and plough and Roman road and daisied
      bank,
Half-conscious that these barriers over which they
      stride
Are nothing to the barbed wire that has grown round
      their pride.
A. And two there are, as I drive in the city, who suddenly
      perturb—
The one sirening me to draw up by the kerb
The other, as I lean back, my right leg stretched
      creating speed,

Making me catch and stamp, the brakes shrieking,
      pull up dead:
She wears silk stockings taunting the winter wind,
He carries a white stick to mark that he is blind.

B. In the country they are still hunting, in the heavy
      shires
Greyness is on the fields and sunset like a line of pyres
Of barbarous heroes smoulders through the ancient air
Hazed with factory dust and, orange opposite, the
      moon's glare,
Goggling yokel-stubborn through the iron trees,
Jeers at the end of us, our bland ancestral ease;
We shall go down like palaeolithic man
Before some new Ice Age or Genghiz Khan.

A. It is time for some new coinage, people have got so old,
Hacked and handled and shiny from pocketing they
      have made bold
To think that each is himself through these accidents,
      being blind
To the fact that they are merely the counters of an
      unknown Mind.

B. A Mind that does not think, if such a thing can be,
Mechanical Reason, capricious Identity.
That I could be able to face this domination nor
      flinch—

A. The tin toys of the hawker move on the pavement
      inch by inch
Not knowing that they are wound up; it is better to
      be so
Than to be, like us, wound up and while running
      down to know—

B. But everywhere the pretence of individuality recurs—
A. Old faces frosted with powder and choked in furs.

B. The jutlipped farmer gazing over the humpbacked
      wall.
A. The commercial traveller joking in the urinal,
B. I think things draw to an end, the soil is stale.
A. And over-elaboration will nothing now avail,
   The street is up again, gas, electricity or drains,
   Ever-changing conveniences, nothing comfortable
      remains
   Un-improved, as flagging Rome improved villa and
      sewer
   (A sound-proof library and a stable temperature).
   Our street is up, red lights sullenly mark
   The long trench of pipes, iron guts in the dark,
   And not till the Goths again come swarming down the
      hill
   Will cease the clangour of the electric drill.
   But yet there is beauty narcotic and deciduous
   In this vast organism grown out of us:
   On all the traffic-islands stand white globes like moons,
   The city's haze is clouded amber that purrs and croons,
   And tilting by the noble curve bus after tall bus comes
   With an osculation of yellow light, with a glory like
      chrysanthemums.
B. The country gentry cannot change, they will die in
      their shoes
   From angry circumstance and moral self-abuse,
   Dying with a paltry fizzle they will prove their lives
      to be
   An ever-diluted drug, a spiritual tautology.
   They cannot live once their idols are turned out,
   None of them can endure, for how could they,
      possibly, without

The flotsam of private property, pekingese and poly-
       anthus,
The good things which in the end turn to poison and
       pus,
Without the bandy chairs and the sugar in the silver
       tongs
And the inter-ripple and resonance of years of dinner-
       gongs?
Or if they could find no more that cumulative proof
In the rain dripping off the conservatory roof?
What will happen when the only sanction the country-
       dweller has—
A. What will happen to us, planked and panelled with
       jazz?
Who go to the theatre where a black man dances like
       an eel,
Where pink thighs flash like the spokes of a wheel,
       where we feel
That we know in advance all the jogtrot and the cake-
       walk jokes,
All the bumfun and the gags of the comedians in
       boaters and toques,
All the tricks of the virtuosos who invert the usual—
B. What will happen to us when the State takes down the
       manor wall,
When there is no more private shooting or fishing,
       when the trees are all cut down,
When faces are all dials and cannot smile or frown—
A. What will happen when the sniggering machine-guns
       in the hands of the young men
Are trained on every flat and club and beauty parlour
       and Father's den?

What will happen when our civilisation like a long
        pent balloon—
B. What will happen will happen; the whore and the
        buffoon
Will come off best; no dreamers, they cannot lose their
        dream
And are at least likely to be reinstated in the new
        régime.
But one thing is not likely—
A.   Do not gloat over yourself
Do not be your own vulture, high on some mountain
        shelf
Huddle the pitiless abstractions bald about the neck
Who will descend when you crumple in the plains a
        wreck.
Over the randy of the theatre and cinema I hear songs
Unlike anything—
B.   The lady of the house poises the silver tongs
And picks a lump of sugar, 'ne plus ultra' she says
'I cannot do otherwise, even to prolong my days'—
A. I cannot do otherwise either, tonight I will book my
        seat—
B. I will walk about the farm-yard which is replete
As with the smell of dung so with memories—
A. I will gorge myself to satiety with the oddities
Of every artiste, official or amateur,
Who has pleased me in my rôle of hero-worshipper
Who has pleased me in my rôle of individual man—
B. Let us lie once more, say 'What we think, we can'
The old idealist lie—
A.   And for me before I die
Let me go the round of the garish glare—
B.   And on the bare and high

18

Places of England, the Wiltshire Downs and the Long
    Mynd
Let the balls of my feet bounce on the turf, my face
    burn in the wind
My eyelashes stinging in the wind, and the sheep like
    grey stones
Humble my human pretensions—

A.   Let the saxophones and the xylophones
And the cult of every technical excellence, the miles of
    canvas in the galleries
And the canvas of the rich man's yacht snapping and
    tacking on the seas
And the perfection of a grilled steak—

B.   Let all these so ephemeral things
Be somehow permanent like the swallow's tangent
    wings:
Goodbye to you, this day remember is Christmas, this
    morn
They say, interpret it your own way, Christ is born.

1933

Their verdure dare not show . . . their verdure dare not
    show . . .
Cant and randy—the seals' heads bobbing in the tide-flow
Between the islands, sleek and black and irrelevant
They cannot depose logically what they want:
Died by gunshot under borrowed pennons,
Sniped from the wet gorse and taken by the limp fins
And slung like a dead seal in a boghole, beaten up
By peasants with long lips and the whisky-drinker's cough.
Park your car in the city of Dublin, see Sackville Street
Without the sandbags in the old photos, meet
The statues of the patriots, history never dies,
At any rate in Ireland, arson and murder are legacies
Like old rings hollow-eyed without their stones
Dumb talismans.
See Belfast, devout and profane and hard,
Built on reclaimed mud, hammers playing in the ship-
    yard.
Time punched with holes like a steel sheet, time
Hardening the faces, veneering with a grey and speckled
    rime
The faces under the shawls and caps:
This was my mother-city, these my paps.
Country of callous lava cooled to stone,
Of minute sodden haycocks, of ship-sirens' moan,
Of falling intonations—I would call you to book
I would say to you, Look;
I would say, This is what you have given me
Indifference and sentimentality
A metallic giggle, a fumbling hand
A heart that leaps to a fife band:

Set these against your water-shafted air
Of amethyst and moonstone, the horses' feet like bells of
        hair
Shambling beneath the orange-cart, the beer-brown
        spring
Guzzling between the heather, the green gush of Irish
        spring.
Cursèd be he that curses his mother. I cannot be
Anyone else than what this land engendered me:
In the back of my mind are snips of white, the sails
Of the Lough's fishing-boats, the bellropes lash their tails
When I would peal my thoughts, the bells pull free—
Memory in apostasy.
I would tot up my factors
But who can stand in the way of his soul's steam-tractors?
I can say Ireland is hooey, Ireland is
A gallery of fake tapestries,
But I cannot deny my past to which my self is wed,
The woven figure cannot undo its thread.
On a cardboard lid I saw when I was four
Was the trade-mark of a hound and a round tower,
And that was Irish glamour, and in the cemetery
Sham Celtic crosses claimed our individuality,
And my father talked about the West where years back
He played hurley on the sands with a stick of wrack.
Park your car in Killarney, buy a souvenir
Of green marble or black bog-oak, run up to Clare,
Climb the cliff in the postcard, visit Galway city,
Romanticise on our Spanish blood, leave ten per cent of
        pity
Under your plate for the emigrant,
Take credit for our sanctity, our heroism and our sterile
        want

Columba Kevin and briny Brandan the accepted names,
Wolfe Tone and Grattan and Michael Collins the
         accepted names,
Admire the suavity with which the architect
Is rebuilding the burnt mansion, recollect
The palmy days of the Horse Show, swank your fill,
But take the Holyhead boat before you pay the bill;
Before you face the consequence
Of inbred soul and climatic maleficence
And pay for the trick beauty of a prism
In drug-dull fatalism.
I will exorcise my blood
And not to have my baby-clothes my shroud
I will acquire an attitude not yours
And become as one of your holiday visitors,
And however often I may come
Farewell, my country, and in perpetuum;
Whatever desire I catch when your wind scours my face
I will take home and put in a glass case
And merely look on
At each new fantasy of badge and gun.
Frost will not touch the hedge of fuchsias,
The land will remain as it was,
But no abiding content can grow out of these minds
Fuddled with blood, always caught by blinds;
The eels go up the Shannon over the great dam;
You cannot change a response by giving it a new name.
Fountain of green and blue curling in the wind
I must go east and stay, not looking behind,
Not knowing on which day the mist is blanket-thick
Nor when sun quilts the valley and quick
Winging shadows of white clouds pass
Over the long hills like a fiddle's phrase.

If I were a dog of sunlight I would bound
From Phoenix Park to Achill Sound,
Picking up the scent of a hundred fugitives
That have broken the mesh of ordinary lives,
But being ordinary too I must in course discuss
What we mean to Ireland or Ireland to us;
I have to observe milestone and curio
The beaten buried gold of an old king's bravado,
Falsetto antiquities, I have to gesture,
Take part in, or renounce, each imposture;
Therefore I resign, good-bye the chequered and the quiet
        hills
The gaudily-striped Atlantic, the linen-mills
That swallow the shawled file, the black moor where half
A turf-stack stands like a ruined cenotaph;
Good-bye your hens running in and out of the white house
Your absent-minded goats along the road, your black cows
Your greyhounds and your hunters beautifully bred
Your drums and your dolled-up Virgins and your ignorant
        dead.

1934

❦ ECLOGUE BY A
FIVE-BARRED GATE

(Death and two Shepherds)

D. There is no way here, shepherds, read the wooden sign,
    Your road is a blind road, all this land is mine.
1. But your fields, mister, would do well for our sheep.
2. They could shelter from the sun where the low hills dip.
D. I have sheep of my own, see them over there.
1. There seems no nater in 'em, they look half dead.
2. They be no South Downs, they look so thin and bare.
D. More than half, shepherds, they are more than half
         dead.
    But where are your own flocks you have been so talk-
        ing of?
1. Right here at our elbow—
2.   Or they was so just now.
D. That's right, shepherd, they was so just now.
    Your sheep are gone, they can't speak for you,
    I must have your credentials, sing me who you are.
1. I am a shepherd of the Theocritean breed,
    Been pasturing my songs, man and boy, this thirty
        year—
2. And for me too my pedigree acceptances
    Have multiplied beside the approved streams.
D. This won't do, shepherds, life is not like that,
    And when it comes to death I may say he is not like
        that.
    Have you never thought of Death?
1.   Only off and on,
    Thanatos in Greek, the accent proparoxytone—

24

2. That's not what he means, he means the thing behind
       the word
   Same as took Alice White the time her had her third—
D. Cut out for once the dialect and the pedantry,
   I thought a shepherd was a poet—
1.   On his flute—
2.   On his oat—
D. I thought he was a poet and could quote the prices
   Of significant living and decent dying, could lay the
       rails level on the sleepers
   To carry the powerful train of abstruse thought—
1. What an idea!
2.   But certainly poets are sleepers,
   The sleeping beauty behind the many-coloured
       hedge—
D. All you do is burke the other and terrible beauty, all
       you do is hedge
   And shirk the inevitable issue, all you do
   Is shear your sheep to stop your ears.
   Poetry you think is only the surface vanity,
   The painted nails, the hips narrowed by fashion,
   The hooks and eyes of words; but it is not that only,
   And it is not only the curer sitting by the wayside,
   Phials on his trestle, his palms grown thin as wafers
   With blessing the anonymous heads;
   And poetry is not only the bridging of two-banked
       rivers.
2. Whoever heard of a river without a further bank?
D. You two never heard of it.
   Tell me now, I have heard the cuckoo, there is tar on
       your shoes,
   I surmise that spring is here—
2.   Spring be here truly,

On Bank Holiday I wore canvas shoes,
Could feel the earth—

D.   And that being so, tell me
Don't you ever feel old?

2.   There's a question now.

1. It is a question we all have to answer,
And I may say that when I smell the beans or hear
            the thrush
I feel a wave intensely bitter-sweet and topped with
            silver—

D. There you go again, your self-congratulation
Blunts all edges, insulates with wool
No spark of reality possible.
Can't you peel off for even a moment that conscious
            face.
All time is not your tear-off jotter, you cannot afford
            to scribble
So many so false answers.
This escapism of yours is blasphemy,
An immortal cannot blaspheme for one way or another
His trivialities will pattern in the end;
But for you your privilege and panic is to be mortal
And with Here and Now for your anvil
You must strike while the iron is hot—

2.   He is an old man,
That is why he talks so.

D.   Can't you understand me?
Look, I will set you a prize like any of your favourites,
Like any Tityrus or tired Damon;
Sing me, each in turn, what dream you had last night
And if either's dream rings true, to him I will open
            my gate:

2. Ho, here's talking.

26

1.   Let me collect myself.
D. Collect yourself in time for if you win my prize—
2. I'm going to sing first, I had a rare dream.
1. Your dream is nothing—
D.   The more nothing the better.
1. My dream will word well—
2.   But not wear well—
D. No dreams wear at all as dreams.
    Water appears tower only while in well—
    All from the same comes, the same drums sound
    In the pulsation of all the bulging suns,
    And no clock whatever, while winding or running
        down,
    Makes any difference to time however the long-legged
        weights
    Straggle down the cottage wall or the child grows
        leggy too—
1. I do not like your talking.
2.   It gives giddiness
    Like the thrumming of the telephone wires in an east
        wind
    With the bellyache and headache and nausea.
D. It is not my nature to talk, so sing your pieces
    And I will try, what is repugnant too, to listen.
1. Last night as the bearded lips of sleep
    Closed with the slightest sigh on me and I sank
        through the blue soft caves
    Picked with light delicate as the chink of coins
    Or stream on the pebbles I was caught by hands
    And a face was swung in my eyes like a lantern
    Swinging on the neck of a snake.
    And that face I knew to be God and I woke,
    And now I come to look at yours, stranger,

There is something in the lines of it—
D.   Your dream, shepherd,
Is good enough of its kind. Now let us hear yours.
2. Well, I dreamt it was a hot day, the territorials
    Were out on melting asphalt under the howitzers,
    The brass music bounced on the houses. Come
    I heard cry as it were a water-nymph, come and fulfil
        me
    And I sped floating, my feet plashing in the tops of
        the wheat
    But my eyes were blind,
    I found her with my hands lying on the drying hay,
    Wet heat in the deeps of the hay as my hand delved,
    And I possessed her, gross and good like the hay,
    And she went and my eyes regained sight and the sky
        was full of ladders
    Angels ascending and descending with a shine like
        mackerel—
    Now I come to tell it it sounds nonsense.
D. Thank you, gentlemen, these two dreams are good,
    Better than your daytime madrigals.
    If you really wish I will give you both the prize,
    But take another look at my land before you choose
        it.
1. It looks colder now.
2.   The sheep have not moved.
1. I have a fancy there is no loving there
    Even among sheep.
D.   They do not breed or couple.
1 & 2. And what about us, shall we enjoy it there?
D. *Enjoy what where?*
2.   Why, life in your land.
D. I will open this gate that you may see for yourselves.

1. You go first.
2.   Well, you come too.
1 & 2.   We will go together to these pastures new . . .
D. So; they are gone; life in my land . . .
     There is no life as there is no land.
     They are gone and I am alone
     With a gate the façade of a mirage.

                                        1934

Shuttles of trains going north, going south, drawing
    threads of blue,
The shining of the lines of trams like swords,
Thousands of posters asserting a monopoly of the good,
    the beautiful, the true,
Crowds of people all in the vocative, you and you,
The haze of the morning shot with words.

Yellow sun comes white off the wet streets but bright
Chromium yellows in the gay sun's light,
Filleted sun streaks the purple mist,
Everything is kissed and reticulated with sun
Scooped-up and cupped in the open fronts of shops
And bouncing on the traffic which never stops.

And the street fountain blown across the square
Rainbow-trellises the air and sunlight blazons
The red butcher's and scrolls of fish on marble slabs,
Whistled bars of music crossing silver sprays
And horns of cars, touché, touché, rapiers' retort, a
    moving cage,
A turning page of shine and sound, the day's maze.

But when the sun goes out, the streets go cold, the
    hanging meat
And tiers of fish are colourless and merely dead,
And the hoots of cars neurotically repeat and the
    tiptoed feet
Of women hurry and falter whose faces are dead;
And I see in the air but not belonging there
The blown grey powder of the fountain grey as the ash
That forming on a cigarette covers the red.

1935

Among these turf-stacks graze no iron horses
Such as stalk, such as champ in towns and the soul of
    crowds,
Here is no mass-production of neat thoughts
No canvas shrouds for the mind nor any black hearses:
The peasant shambles on his boots like hooves
Without thinking at all or wanting to run in grooves.

But those who lack the peasant's conspirators,
The tawny mountain, the unregarded buttress,
Will feel the need of a fortress against ideas and against
    the
Shuddering insidious shock of the theory-vendors,
The little sardine men crammed in a monster toy
Who tilt their aggregate beast against our crumbling
    Troy.

For we are obsolete who like the lesser things
Who play in corners with looking-glasses and beads;
It is better we should go quickly, go into Asia
Or any other tunnel where the world recedes,
Or turn blind wantons like the gulls who scream
And rip the edge off any ideal or dream.

1932

We with our Fair pitched among the feathery clover
Are always cowardly and never sober,
Drunk with steam-organs, thigh-rub and cream-soda
—We cannot remember enemies in this valley.

As chestnut candles turn to conkers, so we
Knock our brains together extravagantly
Instead of planting them to make more trees
—Who have not as yet sampled God's malice.

But to us urchins playing with paint and filth
A prophet scanning the road on the hither hills
Might utter the old warning of the old sin
—Avenging youth threatening an old war.

Crawling down like lava or termites
Nothing seduces, nothing dissolves, nothing affrights
You who scale off masks and smash the purple lights
—But I will escape, with my dog, on the far side of the
　　　Fair.

　　　　　　　　　　　　　　　　　　　　1933

Our half-thought thoughts divide in sifted wisps
Against the basic facts repatterned without pause,
I can no more gather my mind up in my fist
Than the shadow of the smoke of this train upon the
      grass—
This is the way that animals' lives pass.

The train's rhythm never relents, the telephone posts
Go striding backwards like the legs of time to where
In a Georgian house you turn at the carpet's edge
Turning a sentence while, outside my window here,
The smoke makes broken queries in the air.

The train keeps moving and the rain holds off,
I count the buttons on the seat, I hear a shell
Held hollow to the ear, the mere
Reiteration of integers, the bell
That tolls and tolls, the monotony of fear.

At times we are doctrinaire, at times we are frivolous,
Plastering over the cracks, a gesture making good,
But the strength of us does not come out of us.
It is we, I think, are the idols and it is God
Has set us up as men who are painted wood,

And the trains carry us about. But not consistently so,
For during a tiny portion of our lives we are not in trains,
The idol living for a moment, not muscle-bound
But walking freely through the slanting rain,
Its ankles wet, its grimace relaxed again.

All over the world people are toasting the King,
Red lozenges of light as each one lifts his glass,
But I will not give you any idol or idea, creed or king,

I give you the incidental things which pass
Outwards through space exactly as each was.

I give you the disproportion between labour spent
And joy at random; the laughter of the Galway sea
Juggling with spars and bones irresponsibly,
I give you the toy Liffey and the vast gulls,
I give you fuchsia hedges and whitewashed walls.

I give you the smell of Norman stone, the squelch
Of bog beneath your boots, the red bog-grass,
The vivid chequer of the Antrim hills, the trough of dark
Golden water for the cart-horses, the brass
Belt of serene sun upon the lough.

And I give you the faces, not the permanent masks,
But the faces balanced in the toppling wave—
His glint of joy in cunning as the farmer asks
Twenty per cent too much, or a girl's, forgetting to be
        suave,
A tiro choosing stuffs, preferring mauve.

And I give you the sea and yet again the sea's
Tumultuous marble.
With Thor's thunder or taking his ease akimbo
Lumbering torso, but finger-tips a marvel
Of surgeon's accuracy.

I would like to give you more but I cannot hold
This stuff within my hands and the train goes on,
I know that there are further syntheses to which,
As you have perhaps, people at last attain
And find that they are rich and breathing gold.

1934

34

LES SYLPHIDES

Life in a day: he took his girl to the ballet;
Being shortsighted himself could hardly see it --
  The white skirts in the grey
  Glade and the swell of the music
  Lifting the white sails.

Calyx upon calyx, canterbury bells in the breeze
The flowers on the left mirror to the flowers on the right
  And the naked arms above
  The powdered faces moving
  Like seaweed in a pool.

Now, he thought, we are floating-ageless, oarless-
Now there is no separation, from now on
  You will be wearing white
  Satin and a red sash
  Under the waltzing trees.

But the music stopped, the dancers took their curtain,
The river had come to a lock - a shuffle of programmes-
  And we cannot continue down
  Stream unless we are ready
  To enter the lock and drop.

So they were married- to be the more together -
And found they were never again so much together,
  Divided by the morning tea,
  By the evening paper,
  By children and tradesmen's bills.

Waking at times in the night she found assurance
In his regular breathing but wondered whether
  It was really worth it and where
  The river had flowed away
  And where were the white flowers.

Cuckoo across the poppies
    Making myth—
Simeon on his pillar
    Stands in the air alone.

Without context
    Not looking down,
Personification
    Of distance.

Nothing to be seen
    But a stone posture,
The shape of the song
    Of the cuckoo.

1935

The quietude of a soft wind
Will not rescind
My debts to God, but gentle-skinned
His finger probes. I lull myself
In quiet in diet in riot in dreams,
In dopes in drams in drums in dreams
Till God retire and the door shut.
But
Now I am left in the fire-blaze
The peacefulness of the fire-blaze
Will not erase
My debts to God for His mind strays
Over and under and all ways
All days and always.

1929

Borrowed wings on his ankles,
Carrying a stone death,
The hero entered the hall,
All in the hall looked up,
Their breath frozen on them,
And there was no more shuffle or clatter in the hall at all.

So a friend of a man comes in
And leaves a book he is lending or flowers
And goes again, alive but as good as dead,
And you are left alive, no better than dead,
And you dare not turn the leaden pages of the book or
        touch the flowers, the hooded and arrested hours.

Shut your eyes,
There are suns beneath your lids,
Or look in the looking-glass in the end room—
You will find it full of eyes,
The ancient smiles of men cut out with scissors and kept
        in mirrors.

Ever to meet me comes, in sun or dull,
The gay hero swinging the Gorgon's head
And I am left, with the dull drumming of the sun,
        suspended and dead,
Or the dumb grey-brown of the day is a leper's cloth,
And one feels the earth going round and round the globe
        of the blackening mantle, a mad moth.

1934

Your thoughts make shape like snow; in one night
     only
The gawky earth grows breasts,
Snow's unity engrosses
Particular pettiness of stones and grasses.
But before you proclaim the millennium, my dear,
Consult the barometer—
This poise is perfect but maintained
For one day only.

1933

Down the road someone is practising scales,
The notes like little fishes vanish with a wink of tails,
Man's heart expands to tinker with his car
For this is Sunday morning, Fate's great bazaar,
Regard these means as ends, concentrate on this Now,
And you may grow to music or drive beyond Hindhead
      anyhow,
Take corners on two wheels until you go so fast
That you can clutch a fringe or two of the windy past,
That you can abstract this day and make it to the week of
      time
A small eternity, a sonnet self-contained in rhyme.

But listen, up the road, something gulps, the church spire
Opens its eight bells out, skulls' mouths which will not tire
To tell how there is no music or movement which secures
Escape from the weekday time. Which deadens and
      endures.

1933

The shadows of the bannisters march march,
The lovers linger under the arch,
On the beach the waves creep,
The little boy cannot go to sleep.

He is afraid of God and the Devil—
If he shuts his eyes they will draw level,
So he watches the half-open door and waits
For people on the stairs carrying lights.

Someone comes, carrying a lamp,
The shadows of the bannisters march march,
All is above board, order is restored,
Time on horseback under a Roman arch.

Then the final darkness for eight hours
The murderous grin of toothy flowers,
The tick of his pulse in the pillow, the sick
Vertigo of falling in a fanged pit.

After one perfunctory kiss
His parents snore in conjugal bliss.
The night watchman with crossed thumbs
Grows an idol. The Kingdom comes. . . .

1935

Smoke from the train-gulf hid by hoardings blunders up-
　　ward, the brakes of cars
Pipe as the policeman pivoting round raises his flat hand,
　　bars
With his figure of a monolith Pharaoh the queue of
　　fidgety machines
(Chromium dogs on the bonnet, faces behind the triplex
　　screens),
Behind him the streets run away between the proud glass
　　of shops,
Cubical scent-bottles artificial legs arctic foxes and electric
　　mops,
But beyond this centre the slumward vista thins like a
　　diagram:
There, unvisited, are Vulcan's forges who doesn't care a
　　tinker's damn.

Splayed outwards through the suburbs houses, houses for
　　rest
Seducingly rigged by the builder, half-timbered houses
　　with lips pressed
So tightly and eyes staring at the traffic through bleary
　　haws
And only a six-inch grip of the racing earth in their con-
　　crete claws;
In these houses men as in a dream pursue the Platonic
　　Forms
With wireless and cairn terriers and gadgets approximat-
　　ing to the fickle norms
And endeavour to find God and score one over the neigh-
　　bour

By climbing tentatively upward on jerry-built beauty
and sweated labour.

The lunch hour: the shops empty, shopgirls' faces relax
Diaphanous as green glass, empty as old almanacs
As incoherent with ticketed gewgaws tiered behind
their heads
As the Burne-Jones windows in St. Philip's broken by
crawling leads
Insipid colour, patches of emotion, Saturday thrills
(This theatre is sprayed with 'June') —the gutter take
our old playbills,
Next week-end it is likely in the heart's funfair we
shall pull
Strong enough on the handle to get back our money;
or at any rate it is possible.

On shining lines the trams like vast sarcophagi move
Into the sky, plum after sunset, merging to duck's egg,
barred with mauve
Zeppelin clouds, and Pentecost-like the cars' headlights
bud
Out from sideroads and the traffic signals, crême-de-
menthe or bull's blood,
Tell one to stop, the engine gently breathing, or to go on
To where like black pipes of organs in the frayed and
fading zone
Of the West the factory chimneys on sullen sentry will
all night wait
To call, in the harsh morning, sleep-stupid faces
through the daily gate.

1933

42

(Even so it is not so easy to be dead)

As those who are not athletic at breakfast day by day
Employ and enjoy the sinews of others vicariously,
Shielded by the upheld journal from their dream-
      puncturing wives
And finding in the printed word a multiplication of their
      lives,
So we whose senses give us things misfelt and misheard
Turn also, for our adjustment, to the pretentious word
Which stabilises the light on the sun-fondled trees
And, by photographing our ghosts, claims to put us at
      our ease;
Yet even so, no matter how solid and staid we contrive
Our reconstructions, even a still life is alive
And in your Chardin the appalling unrest of the soul
Exudes from the dried fish and the brown jug and the
      bowl.

                         1933

Upon this beach the falling wall of the sea
Explodes its drunken marble
Amid gulls' gaiety.

Which evercrumbling masonry, cancelling sum,
No one by any device can represent
In any medium.

Turn therefore inland, tripper, foot on the sea-holly,
Forget those waves' monstrous fatuity
And boarding bus be jolly.

1932

The room was suddenly rich and the great bay-window
      was
Spawning snow and pink roses against it
Soundlessly collateral and incompatible:
World is suddener than we fancy it.

World is crazier and more of it than we think,
Incorrigibly plural. I peel and portion
A tangerine and spit the pips and feel
The drunkenness of things being various.

And the fire flames with a bubbling sound for world
Is more spiteful and gay than one supposes—
On the tongue on the eyes on the ears in the palms of
      one's hands—
There is more than glass between the snow and the huge
      roses.

                          1935

The hard cold fire of the northerner
Frozen into his blood from the fire in his basalt
Glares from behind the mica of his eyes
And the salt carrion water brings him wealth.

Down there at the end of the melancholy lough
Against the lurid sky over the stained water
Where hammers clang murderously on the girders
Like crucifixes the gantries stand.

And in the marble stores rubber gloves like polyps
Cluster, celluloid, painted ware, glaring
Metal patents, parchment lampshades, harsh
Attempts at buyable beauty.

In the porch of the chapel before the garish Virgin
A shawled factory-woman as if shipwrecked there
Lies a bunch of limbs glimpsed in the cave of gloom
By us who walk in the street so buoyantly and glib.

Over which country of cowled and haunted faces
The sun goes down with a banging of Orange drums
While the male kind murders each its woman
To whose prayer for oblivion answers no Madonna.

1931

Our April must replenish the delightful wells,
Bucket's lip dipping, light on the sleeping cells,
Man from his vigil in the wintry chapel
Will card his skin with accurate strigil.
O frivolous and astringent spring
We never come full circle, never remember
Self behind self years without number,
A series of dwindling mirrors, but take a tangent line
And start again. Our April must replenish
Our bank-account of vanity and give our doors a coat
      of varnish.
Leave the tedium of audits and of finding correct
For the gaiety of places where people collect
For the paper rosettes of the stadium and the plaudits.
And you, let you paint your face and sleek your leg
      with silk
Which is your right to do
As gay trams run on rails and cows give milk.
Sharp sun-strop, surface-gloss, and momentary caprice
These are what we cherish
Caring not if the bridges and the embankments
Of past and future perish and cease;
Before the leaves grow heavy and the good days vanish
Hold out your glasses which our April must replenish.

1934

The trains pass and the trains pass, chains of lighted
   windows,
A register in an unknown language
For these are the trains in which one never goes.

The familiar rhythm but the unknown implications
Delight like a dead language
Which never shocks us by banal revelations.

So listening for the night express coming down the way
I receive the expected whistle of the engine
Sharp and straight on the ear like stigmata.

1933

Bird-song and postman's whistle
Cross-stitch the morning airs,
The days repeat, the pages flutter in the wind,
The moving stairs
Carry our dreams down as we go up
Magnates and navvies, clerks and lovers
Go up and out to ledgers and levers
And blind men's fingers vision wicker chairs.

Her feathered mules lay on the Persian mat—
What thoughts are these
That Balzac was a gross peasant
And Christina Rossetti suffered from Graves' disease
(Each walks within a ring of dancing hands
That no one sees) ?

But as she stepped out of the crackling silk
And moved her head
Into the shaft of twinkling dust
Many hands, coming out of the air,
Like skimming milk
Stroked ominously her glossed hair.

The paper says a marriage has been arranged—
 Look up their addresses, I never remember addresses,
 They have so many friends . . . Tudor . . . with roses.

The paper says a War—
 You tall young man with a bouquet of black roses
 I know what you are looking for,
 Here is a book with all their addresses.

1935

I do not want to be reflective any more
Envying and despising unreflective things
Finding pathos in dogs and undeveloped handwriting
And young girls doing their hair and all the castles of sand
Flushed, by the children's bedtime, level with the shore.

The tide comes in and goes out again, I do not want
To be always stressing either its flux or its permanence,
I do not want to be a tragic or philosophic chorus
But to keep my eye only on the nearer future
And after that let the sea flow over us.

Come then all of you, come closer, form a circle
Join hands and make believe that joined
Hands will keep away the wolves of water
Who howl along our coast. And be it assumed
That no one hears them among the talk and laughter.

1934

The shutter of time darkening ceaselessly
Has whisked away the foam of may and elder
And I realise how now, as every year before,
Once again the gay months have eluded me.

For the mind, by nature stagey, welds its frame
Tomb-like around each little world of a day;
We jump from picture to picture and cannot follow
The living curve that is breathlessly the same.

While the lawn-mower sings moving up and down
Spirting its little fountain of vivid green,
I, like Poussin, make a still-bound fête of us
Suspending every noise, of insect or machine.

Garlands at a set angle that do not slip,
Theatrically (and as if for ever) grace
You and me and the stone god in the garden
And Time who also is shown with a stone face.

But all this is a dilettante's lie
Time's face is not stone nor still his wings,
Our mind, being dead, wishes to have time die
For we being ghosts cannot catch hold of things.

1933

❧ AUBADE

Having bitten on life like a sharp apple
Or, playing it like a fish, been happy,

Having felt with fingers that the sky is blue,
What have we after that to look forward to?

Not the twilight of the gods but a precise dawn
Of sallow and grey bricks, and newsboys crying war.

1934

Just as those who gaze get higher than those who climb
A paradox unfolds on any who can tamper with time.
Where bus encumbers upon bus and fills its slot
Speed up the traffic in a quick motion film of thought
Till bus succeeds bus so identically sliding through
That you cannot catch the fraction of a chink between
      the two;
But they all go so fast, bus after bus, day after day,
Year after year, that you cannot mark any headway,
But the whole stream of traffic seems to crawl
Carrying its dead boulders down a glacier wall
And we who have always been haunted by the fear of
      becoming stone
Cannot bear to watch that catafalque creep down.
Therefore turn we away to seemingly slower things
And rejoice there to have found the speed of fins and
      wings
In the minnow-twistings of the latinist who alone
Nibbles and darts through the shallows of the lexicon
Or among plate-glass cases in sombre rooms where
Eyes appraise the glazen life of majolica ware
Or where a gardener with trowel and rheumatic pains
Pumps up the roaring sap of vegetables through their
      veins.

1933

53

The small householder now comes out warily
Afraid of the barrage of sun that shouts cheerily,
Spring is massing forces, birds wink in air,
The battlemented chestnuts volley green fire,
The pigeons banking on the wind, the hoots of cars,
Stir him to run wild, gamble on horses, buy cigars;
Joy lies before him to be ladled and lapped from his hand—
Only that behind him, in the shade of his villa, memories
    stand
Breathing on his neck and muttering that all this has
    happened before,
Keep the wind out, cast no clout, try no unwarranted
    jaunts untried before,
But let the spring slide by nor think to board its car
For it rides West to where the tangles of scrap-iron are;
Do not walk, these voices say, between the bucking
    clouds alone
Or you may loiter into a suddenly howling crater, or fall,
    jerked back, garrotted by the sun.

1933

Museums offer us, running from among the 'buses,
A centrally heated refuge, parquet floors and sarcopha-
      guses,
Into whose tall fake porches we hurry without a sound
Like a beetle under a brick that lies, useless, on the ground.
Warmed and cajoled by the silence the cowed cypher
      revives,
Mirrors himself in the cases of pots, paces himself by
      marble lives,
Makes believe it was he that was the glory that was Rome,
Soft on his cheek the nimbus of other people's martyrdom,
And then returns to the street, his mind an arena where
      sprawls
Any number of consumptive Keatses and dying Gauls.

1933

In a between world, a world of amber,
The old cat on the sand-warm window-sill
Sleeps on the verge of nullity.

Spring sunshine has a quality
Transcending rooks and the hammering   .
Of those who hang new pictures,
Asking if it is worth it
To clamour and caw, to add stick to stick for ever.

If it is worth while really
To colonise any more the already populous
Tree of knowledge, to portion and reportion
Bits of broken knowledge brittle and dead,
Whether it would not be better
To hide one's head in the warm sand of sleep
And be embalmed without hustle or bother.

The rooks bicker heckle bargain always
And market carts lumber—
Let me in the calm of the all-humouring sun
Also indulge my humour
And bury myself beyond creaks and cawings
In a below world, a bottom world of amber.

1929

'. . . *vitreamque Circen*'

Something of glass about her, of dead water,
Chills and holds us,
Far more fatal than painted flesh or the lodestone
        of live hair
This despair of crystal brilliance.
Narcissus' error
Enfolds and kills us—
Dazed with gazing on that unfertile beauty
Which is our own heart's thought.
Fled away to the beasts
One cannot stop thinking; Timon
Kept on finding gold.
In parrot-ridden forest or barren coast
A more importunate voice than bird or wave
Escutcheoned on the air with ice letters
Seeks and, of course, finds us
        (Of course, being our echo).

Be brave, my ego, look into your glass
And realise that that never-to-be-touched
Vision is your mistress.

                                    1931

Beyond the dykes of cloud and steel spikes of air
The sun's breathing golden prickling fur
Over a vibrant belly warned us
Leap the beast will sometime
Breaking every bridge of the well-worn thoroughfare
Of the zodiac. Gone the fawning yawning purr
Changed for a foam-flash. Gone the indolent industry
That padded round the treadmill, raised the crops
And helped to work the tides. Look up and see
Fiery now . . . how he angrily
Flicks his tongue hungry around his chops.

Blood slavers over the evening sky;
Bees are at compline, not knowing that soon
An end is set to respectability.
On the skyline shaggy spears of grass
Itch ominously and the moon
Limps on a crutch whose ferrule taps to us
Doom (if rightly we decodify) .

Still we are happy even if our nerves
Twitch now and again as the grasses do.
We know that we only live on sufferance
And that however well this star-seat serves
Our purpose as trapezists for this once,
In any case the rope is wearing through.
Tom Tom Terry, Tom Tom Terry.
The glutton tit swings in the cocoanut
In the equinoctial gale.
This circus-job means death sooner or later
From wild beasts or fire among the tinsel.
Tom Tom Terry, Tom Tom Terry.

1929

Barometer of my moods today, mayfly,
Up and down one among a million, one
The same at best as the rest of the jigging mayflies,
One only day of May alive beneath the sun.

The yokels tilt their pewters and the foam
Flowers in the sun beside the jewelled water.
Daughter of the South, call the sunbeams home
To nest between your breasts. The kingcups
Ephemeral are gay gulps of laughter.

Gulp of yellow merriment; cackle of ripples;
Lips of the river that pout and whisper round the reeds.
The mayfly flirting and posturing over the water
Goes up and down in the lift so many times for fun.

'When we are grown up we are sure to alter
Much for the better, to adopt solider creeds;
The Kingcup will cease proffering his cup
And the foam will have blown from the beer and the heat
        no longer dance
And the lift lose fascination and the May
Change her tune to June—but the trouble with us may-
        flies
Is that we never have the chance to be grown up.'

They never have the chance, but what of time they have
They stretch out taut and thin and ringing clear;
So we, whose strand of life is not much more,
Let us too make our time elastic and
Inconsequently dance above the dazzling wave.

Nor put too much on the sympathy of things,
The dregs of drink, the dried cups of flowers,
The pathetic fallacy of the passing hours
When it is we who pass them—hours of stone
Long rows of granite sphinxes looking on.

It is we who pass them, we the circus masters
Who make the mayflies dance, the lapwings lift their
  crests,
The show will soon shut down, its gay-rags gone,
But when this summer is over let us die together,
I want always to be near your breasts.

1929-34

Tonight is so coarse with chocolate
    The wind blowing from Bournville
That I hanker after the Atlantic
    With a frivolous nostalgia
Like that which film-fans feel
    For their celluloid abstractions
The nifty hero and the deathless blonde
    And find escape by proxy
From the eight-hour day or the wheel
    Of work and bearing children.

If God is boundless as the sea or sky
The eye bounds both of them and Him,
We always have the horizon
Not to swim to but to see:
God is seen with shape and limit
More purple towards the rim,
This segment of His infinite extension
Is all the God of Him for me.

And you too, my love, my limit,
So palpable and your hair shot with red—
I do not want a hundred wives or lives
Any more than I want to be too well-read
Or have money like the sand or ability like the hydra's
    heads
To flicker the tongues of self-engendering power,
I want a sufficient sample, the exact and framed
Balance of definite masses, the islanded hour.

I would pray for that island; mob mania in the air,
I cannot assume their easy bravery

Drugged with a slogan, chewing the old lie
That parallel lines will meet at infinity;
As I walk on the shore of the regular and rounded sea
I would pray off from my son the love of that infinite
Which is too greedy and too obvious; let his Absolute
Like any four-walled house be put up decently.

Let us turn to homeliness,
Born in the middle of May
Let him accumulate, corroborate while he may
The blessedness of fact
Which lives in the dancing atom and the breathing
      trees
And everywhere except in the fancy of man
Who daubs his slush on the hawthorn and the may.

Let him have five good senses
The feeling for symmetry
And the sense of the magnet,
His mind deft and unflustered
To change gear easily
And let not the blasphemy
Of dusty words deceive him.

May he hit the golden mean
Which contains the seasonal extreme,
May he riot in the diving sun
And die in the crystal dream,
May his good deeds flung forth
Like boomerangs return
To wear around his neck
As beads of definite worth.

May he pick up daintily
The ambiguous joys,
As a bee in May the blossom of fruit
Cross-fertilise his data and distil
From the drum balalaika fiddle and organ
From sun's gunnery splintering glass
More than the twanging dazzle or the dazzling noise.

To get permanence, to hear the personance
Of all the water-gullies and blackbirds' songs
Drained off or died twenty years back
To make one's flesh of them and so renounce the mask
Of the sham soul, the cask bobbing empty
On leaden waves, the veneer the years crack.

To ride two horses at once, a foot on each
Tilting outward on space abstract and packed
With the audience of the dead and the unborn,
To pay his debts to each
To beach his boat so that others can use it
To throw his bread on the waters, the best deposit.

That people are lovable is a strange discovery
And there are many conflicting allegiances;
The pedals of a chance bicycle
Make a gold shower turning in the sun,
Trains leave in all directions on wild rails
And for every act determined on and won
There is a possible world denied and lost.

Do not then turn maudlin or weathercock,
We must cut the throat of the hour
That it may not haunt us because our sentiments
Continued its existence to pollute
Its essence; bottled time turns sour upon the sill.

63

The children play in the park; the ducklings
Rise and scurry on the water, a car
Changes down, the sandwichmen
Move up and down with the never-changing news.
Do not brood too much on the forking paths.

The leaves dark green on top, light green under, seas of
      green
Had brought him on full flood, the colour laid on in slices
As by a mason's trowel or ice cream in sliders
Bought in dusty streets under the yellow-green beeches,
A little while ago the green was only peppered
But now we gape at a wealthy wave and a tidal tower of
      green.

Coral azalea and scarlet rhododendron
Syringa and pink horse-chestnut and laburnum
Solid as temples, niched with the song of birds,
Widen the eyes and nostrils, demand homage of words.
And we have to turn from them,
Compose ourselves, fit out an ethic:
Have I anything to hand my son,
Scarab or compass for his journey?

Only so far, so far as I can find, symbols;
No decalogue, no chemical formula;
Unanalysed scent and nose, the fly on the pane,
The tulips banked on the glass-and-black hearse
A memory of a cock crowing in the dark like a curse
The remembered hypnotism of an aeroplane in June—

Watching the cricket from between
Slabs of green and slabs of blue and slowly ladled clouds
We looked at the sky through straw hats,
The sky was turned into black and white small stars.

Then came, southward as always, the angel
His song like the heat dancing on the gravel
High above the bat-chock and the white umpires
Moving south while the clapping of a run turns chill in
         echo
And his own drone is whittled to the point of a pin
So that dozing boys fumble the ghost of sound.

But this identical sound the then epitome
Of summer's athletic ease and the smell of cut grass
Will sometime be our augury of war
When these tiny flies like nibs will calmly draw our death
A dipping gradient on the graph of Europe
And over the hairy flatnesses of Russia
This sound when we have died will linger to a wisp
And the endless corn wave tiredly.

Humming and buzzing, the bomber and the fly on the
         pane
And the telephone wires hung on dead pines,
In Ireland once a string of bright-red haws
Hung, thrown up by children, on those wires:
Not to hang so, O God, between your iron spires!
The town-dweller like a rabbit in a greengrocer's
Who was innocent and integral once
Now, red with slit guts, hangs by the heels
Hangs by the heels gut-open against the fog
Between two spires that are not conscious of him.

Therefore let not my son, halving the truth
Be caught between jagged edges;
And let him not falsify the world
By taking it to pieces;
The marriage of Cause and Effect, Form and Content
Let him not part asunder.

Wisdom for him in the time of tulips
Monastic repose, martial élan,
Then the opening mouth a dragon or a voluptuary—
These moments let him retain like limbs
His time not crippled by flaws of faith or memory.

In the Birmingham Market Hall at this time
There are horseshoe wreaths of mauve stock
Fixed with wire and nailed with pale pink roses
The tribute to a life that ran on standard wheels—
May his life be more than this matter of wheels and
        wire.

I remember all the houses where parents
Have reared their children to be parents
(Cut box and privet and the parrot's voice)
To be clerks to total the flow of alien money
To be florists to design these wreaths and wedding
        bouquets.

I cannot draw up any code
      There are too many qualifications
Too many asterisk asides
      Too many crosses in the margin
But as others, forgetting the others,
      Run after the nostrums
Of science art and religion
      So would I mystic and maudlin
Dream of the both real and ideal
      Breakers of ocean.
I must put away this drug.

Must become the migrating bird following felt routes
The comet's superficially casual orbit kept

Not self-abandoning to sky-blind chutes
To climb miles and kiss the miles of foam
For nothing is more proud than humbly to accept
And without soaring or swerving win by ignoring
The endlessly curving sea and so come to one's home.

And so come to one's peace while the yellow waves are
    roaring.

1934

II. EARLY POEMS:

From *Blind Fireworks*, published 1929

The glass is going down. The sun
Is going down. The forecasts say
It will be warm, with frequent showers.
We ramble down the showery hours
And amble up and down the day.
Mary will wear her black goloshes
And splash the puddles on the town;
And soon on fleets of macintoshes
The rain is coming down, the frown
Is coming down of heaven showing
A wet night coming, the glass is going
Down, the sun is going down.

1926

Trains came threading quietly through my dozing child-
    hood,
Gentle murmurs nosing through a summer quietude,
Drawing in and out, in and out, their smoky ribbons,
Parting now and then, and launching full-rigged galleons
And scrolls of smoke that hung in a shifting epitaph.
Then distantly the noise declined like a descending graph,
Sliding downhill gently to the bottom of the distance
(For now all things are there that all were here once) ;
And so we hardly noticed when that metal murmur came
But it brought us assurance and comfort all the same,
And in the early night they soothed us to sleep,
And the chain of the rolling wheels bound us in deep
Till all was broken by that menace from the sea,
The steel-bosomed siren calling bitterly.

1926

❦ CANDLE POEM

I have no clock, yet I can hear
The minutes pass while I sit here
Tired but free from tedium
And mark the waning cylinder.

To-morrow will be another day,
And to-day will then be yesterday,
To click the bonds of business
From Saturday to Saturday.

Another night will follow, but
My candle will then be a candle butt
And the door that is day and day's division
Will have opened once and shut.

Close your armoured books and mark
The waning cylinder that drips
Fluid time from pallid lips,
Making an island in the dark.

This island is too small, I fear;
Dark horses fret away the shore,
And I can build no breakwater
But only close a desperate ear
And mark the waning cylinder.

1927

In this evening room there is no stir, no fuss;
The silken shade of the oil-light is diaphanous,
And so come other noises through the noise of the clock
Transparent as the shade, as a girl's frock.
There is no crease, no fold ruffling the room at all;
The glass fringe of the shade seems a summer waterfall,
Like August insects purring over mown grass
The flames blend and pass, incend and end and pass.
Like the calm blue marriage of the sky and sea,
Or a blue-veiled Madonna beaming vacancy,
See that Madonna snuff out the shaded light
And stroke with soothing hand asleep the night.

1927

74

III. LATER POEMS

The sunlight on the garden
Hardens and grows cold,
We cannot cage the minute
Within its nets of gold;
When all is told
We cannot beg for pardon.

Our freedom as free lances
Advances towards its end;
The earth compels, upon it
Sonnets and birds descend;
And soon, my friend,
We shall have no time for dances.

The sky was good for flying
Defying the church bells
And every evil iron
Siren and what it tells:
The earth compels,
We are dying, Egypt, dying

And not expecting pardon,
Hardened in heart anew,
But glad to have sat under
Thunder and rain with you,
And grateful too
For sunlight on the garden.

1937

With all this clamour for progress
This hammering out of new phases and gadgets, new
        trinkets and phrases
I prefer the automatic, the reflex, the cliché of velvet.
The foreseen smile, sexual, maternal, or hail-fellow-met
The cat's fur sparking under your hand
The indolent delicacy of your hand
These fish coming in to the net
I can see them coming for yards
The way that you answer, the way that you dangle your
        foot
These fish that are rainbow and fat
One can catch in the hand and caress and return to the
        pool.
So five minutes spent at a bar
Watching the fish coming in, as you parry and shrug
This is on me or this is on me,
Or an old man momentously sharpens a pencil as though
He were not merely licking his fur like a cat—
The cat's tongue curls to the back of its neck, the fish swivel
        round by the side of their tails, on the abbey the
        arrows of gold
On the pinnacles shift in the wind—
This is on me this time
Watch how your flattery logic seduction or wit
Elicit the expected response
Each tiny hammer of the abbey chime
Beating on the outer shell of the eternal bell
Which hangs like a Rameses, does not deign to move
For Mahomet comes to the mountain and the fish come to
        the bell.

78

What will you have now? The same again?
A finger can pull these ropes,
A gin and lime or a double Scotch
Watch the response, the lifting wrist the clink and smile
The fish come in, the hammered notes come out
From a filigree gothic trap.
These are the moments that are anaplerotic, these are
        the gifts to be accepted
Remembering the qualification
That everything is not true to type like these
That the pattern and the patina of these
Are superseded in the end.
Stoop your head, follow me through this door
Up the belfry stair.
What do you see in this gloom, this womb of stone?
I see eight bells hanging alone.
Eight black panthers, eight silences
On the outer shell of which our fingers via hammers
Rapping with an impertinent precision
Have made believe that this was the final music.
Final as if finality was the trend of fish
That always seek the net
As if finality was the obvious gag
The audience laughing in anticipation
As if finality was the angled smile
Drawn from the dappled stream of casual meetings
(Yet oh thank God for such)
But there is this much left over
There is very much left over:
The Rameses, the panther, the two-ton bell
Will never move his sceptre
Never spring, never swing
No, no, he will never move. . .

What will you have, my dear? The same again?
Two more double Scotch, watch the approved response
This is the preferred mode
I have shut the little window that looks up the road
Towards the tombs of the kings
For I have heard that you meet people walking in granite
I have shut up the gates under padlock
For fear of wild beasts
And I have shut my ears to the possible peal of bells,
Every precaution—
What will you have, my dear? The same again?
Count up our fag-ends
This year next year sometime never
Next year is this year, sometime is next time, never is some-
        time
Never is the Bell, Never is the Panther, Never is Rameses
Oh the cold stone panic of Never—
The ringers are taking off their coats, the panther crouches
The granite sceptre is very slightly inclining
As our shoes tap against the bar and our glasses
Make two new rings of wet upon the counter
Somewhere behind us stands a man, a counter
A timekeeper with a watch and a pistol
Ready to shoot and with his shot destroy
This whole delightful world of cliché and refrain—
What will you have, my dear? The same again?

1935

No shields now
  Cross the knoll,
The hills are dull
  With leaden shale,
Whose arms could squeeze
  The breath from time
And the climb is long
  From cairn to cairn.

Houses are few
  But decorous
In a ruined land
  Of sphagnum moss;
Corrugated iron
  Farms inherit
The spirit and phrase
  Of ancient sagas

Men have forgotten
  Anger and ambush,
To make ends meet
  Their only business:
The lover riding
  In the lonely dale
Hears the plover's
  Single pipe

And feels perhaps
  But undefined
The drift of death
  In the sombre wind

Deflating the trim
 Balloon of lust
In a grey storm
 Of dust and grit.

So we who have come
 As trippers North
Have minds no match
 For this land's girth;
The glacier's licking
 Tongues deride
Our pride of life,
 Our flashy songs.

But the people themselves
 Who live here
Ignore the brooding
 Fear, the sphinx;
And the radio
 With tags of tune
Defies their pillared
 Basalt crags.

Whose ancestors
 Thought that at last
The end would come
 To a blast of horns
And gods would face
 The worst in fight,
Vanish in the night
 The last, the first

Night which began
    Without device
In ice and rocks,
    No shade or shape;
Grass and blood,
    The strife of life,
Were an interlude
    Which soon must pass

And all go back
    Relapse to rock
Under the shawl
    Of the ice-caps,
The cape which night
    Will spread to cover
The world when the living
    Flags are furled.

1936

The Junes were free and full, driving through tiny
Roads, the mudguards brushing the cowparsley,
Through fields of mustard and under boldly embattled
    Mays and chestnuts

Or between beeches verdurous and voluptuous
Or where broom and gorse beflagged the chalkland—
All the flare and gusto of the unenduring
    Joys of a season

Now returned but I note as more appropriate
To the maturer moods impending thunder
With an indigo sky and the garden hushed except for
    The treetops moving.

Then the curtains in my room blow suddenly inward,
The shrubbery rustles, birds fly heavily homeward,
The white flowers fade to nothing on the trees and rain
    comes
    Down like a dropscene.

Now there comes the catharsis, the cleansing downpour
Breaking the blossoms of our overdated fancies
Our old sentimentality and whimsicality
    Loves of the morning.

Blackness at half-past eight, the night's precursor,
Clouds like falling masonry and lightning's lavish
Annunciation, the sword of the mad archangel
    Flashed from the scabbard.

If only now you would come and dare the crystal
Rampart of rain and the bottomless moat of thunder,
If only now you would come I should be happy
      Now if now only.

                       1937

The heated minutes climb
The anxious hill,
The tills fill up with cash,
The tiny hammers chime
The bells of good and ill,
And the world piles with ash
From fingers killing time.

If you were only here
Among these rocks,
I should not feel the dull
The taut and ticking fear
That hides in all the clocks
And creeps inside the skull—
If you were here, my dear.

If I could make this rhyme
An iron bird
To drop its bombs of lust
And break your guarded time,
Then each exploding word
That loosed your walls to dust
Would compensate my crime.

1937

There are few songs for domesticity
For routine work, money-making or scholarship
Though these are apt for eulogy or for tragedy.

And I would praise our adaptability
Who can spend years and years in offices and beds
Every morning twirling the napkin ring,
A twitter of inconsequent vitality.

And I would praise our inconceivable stamina
Who work to the clock and calendar and maintain
The equilibrium of nerves and notions,
Our mild bravado in the face of time.

Those who ignore disarm. The domestic ambush
The pleated lampshade the defeatist clock
May never be consummated and we may never
Strike on the rock beneath the calm upholstering.

But some though buoyed by habit, though convoyed
By habitual faces and hands that help the food
Or help one with one's coat, have lost their bearings
Struck hidden ice or currents no one noted.

One was found like Judas kissing flowers
And one who sat between the clock and the sun
Lies like a Saint Sebastian full of arrows
Feathered from his own hobby, his pet hours.

1936

Only let it form within his hands once more—
The moment cradled like a brandy glass.
Sitting alone in the empty dining hall . . .
From the chandeliers the snow begins to fall
Piling around carafes and table legs
And chokes the passage of the revolving door.
The last diner, like a ventriloquist's doll
Left by his master, gazes before him, begs:
'Only let it form within my hands once more.'

1937

Upon the decks they take beef tea
    Who are so free, so free, so free,
But down the ladder in the engine-room
    (Doom, doom, doom, doom)
The great cranks rise and fall, repeat,
The great cranks plod with their Assyrian feet
    To match the monotonous energy of the sea.

Back from a journey I require
    Some new desire, desire, desire
But find in the open sea and sun
    None, none, none, none;
The gulls that bank around the mast
Insinuate that nothing we pass is past,
    That all our beginnings were long since begun.

And when I think of you, my dear,
    Who were so near, so near, so near,
The barren skies from wall to wall
    Appal, appal, pall, pall,
The spray no longer gilds the wave,
The sea looks nothing more nor less than a grave
    And the world and the day are grey and that is all.

1937

You who will soon be unrecapturable,
You with your flair for spotted scarves and checks,
The creed I built upon your charm and sex
And *laissez-faire* I find no longer tenable;
But as the loitering senses are incapable
To hold the blend of smells or light in flecks
So knowing you whom no one could annex
Was no more durable than those are durable:
Which is why your trek to not-believed-in lands
Has dislocated the day and quenched the sun
That licked the cornice of my lonely room
Settling now to a grey and reasoned gloom
Where I shall neither recant the minutes gone
Nor fumble for the past with backward hands.

1937

Thank you, my friendly daemon, close to me as my shadow
For the mealy buttercup days in the ancient meadow,
For the days of my 'teens, the sluice of hearing and seeing,
The days of topspin drives and physical well-being.

Thank you, my friend, shorter by a head, more placid
Than me your protégé whose ways are not so lucid,
My animal angel sure of touch and humour
With face still tanned from some primaeval summer.

Thanks for your sensual poise, your gay assurance,
Who skating on the lovely wafers of appearance
Have held my hand, put vetoes upon my reason,
Sent me to look for berries in the proper season.

Some day you will leave me or, at best, less often
I shall sense your presence when eyes and nostrils open,
Less often find your burgling fingers ready
To pick the locks when mine are too unsteady.

Thank you for the times of contact, for the glamour
Of pleasure sold by the clock and under the hammer,
Thank you for bidding for me, for breaking the cordon
Of spies and sentries round the unravished garden.

And thank you for the abandon of your giving,
For seeing in the dark, for making this life worth living.

1937

The dazzle on the sea, my darling,
Leads from the western channel
A carpet of brilliance taking
My leave for ever of the island.

I never shall visit that island
Again with its easy tempo—
The seal sunbathing, the circuit
Of gulls on the wing for garbage.

I go to a different garbage
And scuffle for scraps of notice,
Pretend to ignore the stigma
That stains my life and my leisure.

For fretful even in leisure
I fidget for different values,
Restless as a gull and haunted
By a hankering after Atlantis.

I do not know that Atlantis
Unseen and uncomprehended,
Dimly divined but keenly
Felt with a phantom hunger.

If only I could crush the hunger
If only I could lay the phantom
Then I should no doubt be happy
Like a fool or a dog or a buddha.

O the self-abnegation of Buddha
The belief that is disbelieving

The denial of chiaroscuro
Not giving a damn for existence!

But I would cherish existence
Loving the beast and the bubble
Loving the rain and the rainbow,
Considering philosophy alien.

For all the religions are alien
That allege that life is a fiction,
And when we agree in denial
The cock crows in the morning.

If only I could wake in the morning
And find I had learned the solution,
Wake with the knack of knowledge
Who as yet have only an inkling.

Though some facts foster the inkling—
The beauty of the moon and music,
The routine courage of the worker,
The gay endurance of women,

And you who to me among women
Stand for so much that I wish for,
I thank you, my dear, for the example
Of living in tune and moving.

For few are able to keep moving,
They drag and flag in the traffic;
While you are alive beyond question
Like the dazzle on the sea, my darling.

1937

*Scene: The Arnarvatn Heath. Craven, Ryan, and the
ghost of Grettir. Voice from Europe.*

R.   This is the place, Craven, the end of our way;
         Hobble the horses, we have had a long day.

C.   The lake is said to be full of trout;
         A pity the mist shuts the glacier out.

R.   There used to be swans but the frost last year
         Has brought their numbers down round here.

C.   I like this place. My personal choice
         Is always to avoid the public voice.

R.   You are quite right, Craven. For people like us
         This is an enviable terminus.

C.   To stay here a week like a placid brute
         To explore the country, to fish and shoot.

R.   That would be life, not having to shave,
         Clocking in as a wage-slave.

C.   That would be life, Ryan, that would be life,
         Without kowtowing to boss or wife.

R.   And beside this cold and silicate stream
         To sleep in sheepskin, never dream,

C.   Never dream of the empty church,

R.   Nor of waiting in a familiar porch
         With the broken bellpull, but the name
         Above the door is not the same.

C.   And never wake to the maid's knock

R.   Nor to the sour alarum clock,

C.   Miss the faces fed at eight
         And the daily paper on your plate,

R.   And miss the pile of letters from
         Forgotten Bill and ailing Tom.

94

C.   Stop a moment. I think I hear
      Someone walking over there.
R.   Hell, Craven. Who could it be?
      Except the echo of you and me.
C.   There is someone there just out of sight—
      Will probably camp here to-night.
R.   It is a damn bore anyhow.
      Look. There he is coming now.
      The mist makes him look so big
      And he is limping in one leg.
G.   Good evening, strangers. So you too
      Are on the run? I welcome you.
      I am Grettin Asmundson,
      Dead many years. My day is done.
      But you whose day is sputtering yet—
      I forget. . . . What did I say?
      We forget when we are dead
      The blue and red, the grey and gay.
      Your day spits with a damp wick,
      Will fizzle out if you're not quick.
      Men have been chilled to death who kissed
      Wives of mist, forgetting their own
      Kind who live out of the wind.
      My memory goes, goes—Tell me
      Are there men now whose compass leads
      Them always down forbidden roads?
      Greedy young men who take their pick
      Of what they want but have no luck;
      Who leap the toothed and dour crevasse
      Of death on a sardonic phrase?
      You with crowsfeet round your eyes,
      How are things where you come from?
C.   Things are bad. There is no room
      To move at ease, to stretch or breed—

G. And you with the burglar's underlip,
  In your land do things stand well?
R. In my land nothing stands at all
  But some fly high and some lie low.
G. Too many people. My memory will go,
  Lose itself in the hordes of modern people.
  Memory is words; we remember what others
  Say and record of ourselves—stones with the runes.
  Too many people—sandstorm over the words.
  Is your land also an island?
  There is only hope for people who live upon islands
  Where the Lowest Common labels will not stick
  And the unpolluted hills will hold your echo.
R. I come from an island, Ireland, a nation
  Built upon violence and morose vendettas.
  My diehard countrymen, like drayhorses,
  Drag their ruin behind them.
  Shooting straight in the cause of crooked thinking
  Their greed is sugared with pretence of public
    spirit.
  From all which I am an exile.
C. Yes, we are exiles,
  Gad the world for comfort.
  This Easter I was in Spain, before the Civil War,
  Gobbling the tripper's treats, the local colour,
  Storks over Avila, the coffee-coloured waters of
    Ronda,
  The comedy of the bootblacks in the cafés,
  The legless beggars in the corridors of the trains.
  Dominoes on marble tables, the architecture
  Moorish mudejar churriguerresque,
  The bullfight—the banderillas like Christmas
    candles,

And the scrawled hammer and sickle:
It was all copy—impenetrable surface.
I did not look for the sneer beneath the surface.
Why should I trouble, an addict to oblivion,
Running away from the gods of my own hearth
With no intention of finding gods elsewhere?

R.   And so we came to Iceland—
C.   Our latest joyride.
G.   What have you found in Iceland?
C.   What have we found? More copy, more surface,
Vignettes as they call them, dead flowers in an
      album—
The harmoniums in the farms, the fine-bread and
      pancakes
The pot of ivy trained across the window,
Children in gumboots, girls in black berets.

R.   And dead craters and angled crags.
G.   The crags which saw me jockey doom for twenty
Years from one cold hide-out to another;
The last of the saga heroes
Who had not the wisdom of Njàl or the beauty of
      Gunnar,
I was the doomed tough, disaster kept me witty;
Being born the surly jack, the ne'er-do-well, the
      loiterer,
Hard blows exalted me.
When the man of will and muscle achieves the
      curule chair
He turns to a bully; better is his lot as outlaw,
A wad of dried fish in his belt, a snatch of bilberries
And riding the sullen landscape far from friends
Through the jungle of lava, dales of frozen fancy,
Fording the gletcher, ducking the hard hail,

97

And across the easy pastures, never stopping
To rest among the celandines and bogcotton.
Under a curse I would see eyes in the night,
Always had to move on; craving company
In the end I lived on an island with two others.
To fetch fire I swam the crinkled fjord,
The crags were alive with ravens whose low croak
Told my ears what filtered in my veins—
The sense of doom. I wore it gracefully,
The fatal clarity that would not budge
But without false pride in martyrdom. For I,
Joker and dressy, held no mystic's pose,
Not wishing to die preferred the daily goods
The horse-fight, women's thighs, a joint of meat.

C.   But this dyspeptic age of ingrown cynics
Wakes in the morning with a coated tongue
And whets itself laboriously to labour
And wears a blasé face in the face of death.
Who risk their lives neither to fill their bellies
Nor to avenge an affront nor grab a prize,
But out of bravado or to divert ennui
Driving fast cars and climbing foreign mountains.
Outside the delicatessen shop the hero
With his ribbons and his empty pinned-up sleeve
Cadges for money while with turned-up collars
His comrades blow through brass the London-
      derry Air
And silken legs and swinging buttocks advertise
The sale of little cardboard flags on pins.

G.   Us too they sold
The women and the men with many sheep.
Graft and aggression, legal prevarication
Drove out the best of us,

Secured long life to only the sly and the dumb
To those who would not say what they really
    thought
But got their ends through pretended indifference
And through the sweat and blood of thralls and
    hacks,
Cheating the poor men of their share of drift
The whale on Kaldbak in the starving winter.

R.   And so to-day at Grimsby men whose lives
Are warped in Arctic trawlers load and unload
The shining tons of fish to keep the lords
Of the market happy with cigars and cars.

C.   What is that music in the air—
Organ-music coming from far?

R.   Honeyed music—it sounds to me
Like the Wurlitzer in the Gaiety.

G.   I do not hear anything at all.

C.   Imagine the purple light on the stage,

R.   The melting moment of a stinted age,

C.   The pause before the film again
Bursts in a shower of golden rain.

G.   I do not hear anything at all.

C.   We shall be back there soon, to stand in queues
For entertainment and to work at desks,
To browse round counters of dead books, to pore
On picture catalogues and Soho menus,
To preen ourselves on the reinterpretation
Of the words of obsolete interpreters,
Collate, delete, their faded lives like texts,
Admire Flaubert, Cézanne—the tortured artists—
And leaning forward to knock out our pipes
Into the fire protest that art is good
And gives a meaning and a slant to life.

G.   The dark is falling. Soon the air
       Will stare with eyes, the stubborn ghost
       Who cursed me when I threw him. Must
       The ban go on forever? I,
       A ghost myself, have no claim now to die.

R.   Now I hear the music again—
       Strauss and roses—hear it plain.
       The sweet confetti of music falls
       From the high Corinthian capitals.

C.   Her head upon his shoulder lies. . . .
       Blend to the marrow as the music dies.

G.   Brought up to the rough-house we took offence
          quickly
       Were sticklers for pride, paid for it as outlaws—

C.   Like Cavalcanti, whose hot blood lost him
          Florence

R.   Or the Wild Geese of Ireland in Mid-Europe.
       Let us thank God for valour in abstraction
       For those who go their own way, will not kiss
       The arse of law and order nor compound
       For physical comfort at the price of pride:
       Soldiers of fortune, renegade artists, rebels and
          sharpers
       Whose speech not cramped to Yea and Nay
          explodes
       In crimson oaths like peonies, who brag
       Because they prefer to taunt the mask of God,
       Bid him unmask and die in the living lightning.
       What is that voice maundering, meandering?

Voice. Blues . . . blues . . . high heels and manicured
          hands
       Always self-conscious of the vanity bag
       And puritan painted lips that abnegate desire

And say 'we do not care' . . . 'we do not care'—
I don't care always in the air
Give my hips a shake always on the make
Always on the mend coming around the bend
Always on the dance with an eye to the main
Chance, always taking the floor again—

C.   There was Tchekov,
His haemorrhages drove him out of Moscow,
The life he loved, not born to it, who thought
That when the windows blurred with smoke and
    talk
So that no one could see out, then conversely
The giants of frost and satans of the peasant
Could not look in, impose the evil eye.

R.   There was MacKenna
Spent twenty years translating Greek philosophy,
Ill and tormented, unwilling to break contract,
A brilliant talker who left
The salon for the solo flight of Mind.

G.   There was Onund Treefoot
Came late and lame to Iceland, made his way
Even though the land was bad and the neighbours
    jealous.

C.   There was that dancer
Who danced the war, then falling into coma
Went with hunched shoulders through the ivory
    gate.

R.   There was Connolly,
Vilified now by the gangs of Catholic Action.

G.   There was Egil,
Hero and miser, who when dying blind
Would have thrown his money among the crowd
    to hear

The whole world scuffle for his hoarded gold.
C. And there were many
Whose common sense or sense of humour or mere
Desire for self assertion won them through
R. But not to happiness. Though at intervals
They paused in sunlight for a moment's fusion
With friends or nature till the cynical wind
Blew the trees pale—
Voice.   Blues, blues, sit back, relax,
Let your self-pity swell with the music and clutch
Your tiny lavendered fetishes. Who cares
If floods depopulate China? I don't care
Always in the air sitting among the stars
Among the electric signs among the imported
    wines
Always on the spree climbing the forbidden tree
Tossing the peel of the apple over my shoulder
To see it form the initials of a new intrigue,
G. Runes and runes which no one could decode,
R. Wrong numbers on the 'phone—she never
    answered.
C. And from the romantic grill (Spanish baroque)
Only the eyes looked out which I see now.
G. You see them now?
C.   But seen before as well.
G. And many times to come, be sure of that.
R. I know them too
These eyes which hang in the northern mist, the
    brute
Stare of stupidity and hate, the most
Primitive and false of oracles.
C.   The eyes
That glide like snakes behind a thousand masks—

102

All human faces fit them, here or here:
Dictator, bullying schoolboy, or common lout,
Acquisitive women, financiers, invalids,
Are capable all of that compelling stare,
Stare which betrays the cosmic purposelessness
The nightmare noise of the scythe upon the hone,
Time sharpening his blade among high rocks
      alone.

R.   The face that fate hangs as a figurehead
      Above the truncheon or the nickelled death.

G.   I won the fall. Though cursed for it, I won.

C.   Which is why we honour you who working from
      The common premisses did not end with many
      In the blind alley where the trek began.

G.   Though the open road is hard with frost and dark.

Voice. Hot towels for the men, mud packs for the women
      Will smooth the puckered minutes of your lives.
      I offer you each a private window, a view
      (The leper window reveals a church of lepers).

R.   Do you believe him?

C.   I don't know.
      Do you believe him?

G.   No.
      You cannot argue with the eyes or voice;
      Argument will frustrate you till you die
      But go your own way, give the voice the lie,
      Outstare the inhuman eyes. That is the way.
      Go back to where you came from and do not keep
      Crossing the road to escape them, do not avoid the
        ambush,
      Take sly detours, but ride the pass direct.

C.   But the points of axes shine from the scrub, the
        odds

Are dead against us. There are the lures of women
Who, half alive, invite to a fuller life
And never loving would be loved by others.

R.   Who fortify themselves in pasteboard castles
And plant their beds with the cast-out toys of
     children,
Dead pines with tinsel fruits, nursery beliefs,
And South Sea Island trinkets. Watch their years
The permutations of lapels and gussets,
Of stuffs—georgette or velvet or corduroy—
Of hats and eye-veils, of shoes, lizard or suède,
Of bracelets, milk or coral, of zip bags,
Of compacts, lipstick, eyeshade, and coiffures
All tributary to the wished ensemble,
The carriage of body that belies the soul.

C.   And there are the men who appear to be men of
     sense,
Good company and dependable in a crisis,
Who yet are ready to plug you as you drink
Like dogs who bite from fear; for fear of germs
Putting on stamps by licking the second finger,
For fear of opinion overtipping in bars,
For fear of thought studying stupefaction.
It is the world which these have made where dead
Greek words sprout out in tin on sallow walls—
Clinic or polytechnic—a world of slums
Where any day now may see the Gadarene swine
Rush down the gullets of the London tubes
When the enemy, x or y, let loose their gas.

G.   My friends, hounded like me, I tell you still
Go back to where you belong. I could have fled
To the Hebrides or Orkney, been rich and famous,
Preferred to assert my rights in my own country,

	Mine which were hers for every country stands
	By the sanctity of the individual will.
R.	Yes, he is right.
C.	But we have not his strength,
R.	Could only abase ourselves before the wall
	Of shouting flesh,
C.	Could only offer our humble
	Deaths to the unknown god, unknown but wor-
	shipped,
	Whose voice calls in the sirens of destroyers.
G.	Minute your gesture but it must be made—
	Your hazard, your act of defiance and hymn of
	hate,
	Hatred of hatred, assertion of human values,
	Which is now your only duty.
C.	Is it our only duty?
G.	Yes, my friends.
	What did you say? The night falls now and I
	Must beat the dales to chase my remembered acts.
	Yes, my friends, it is your only duty.
	And, it may be added, it is your only chance.

1936

(A Poem for Hector MacIver)

On those islands
The west wind drops its messages of indolence
No one hurries, the Gulf Stream warms the gnarled
Rampart of gneiss, the feet of the peasant years
Pad up and down their sentry-beat not challenging
Any comer for the password—only Death
Comes through unchallenged in his general's cape.
The houses straggle on the umber moors,
The Aladdin lamp mutters in the boarded room
Where a woman smoors the fire of fragrant peat.
No one repeats the password for it is known,
All is known before it comes to the lips—
Instinctive wisdom. Over the fancy vases
The photos with the wrinkles taken out,
The enlarged portraits of the successful sons
Who married wealth in Toronto or New York,
Cajole the lonely evenings of the old
Who live embanked by memories of labour
And child-bearing and scriptural commentaries.
On those islands
The boys go poaching their ancestral rights—
The Ossianic salmon who take the yellow
Tilt of the river with a magnet's purpose—
And listen breathless to the tales at the ceilidh
Among the peat-smoke and the smells of dung
That fill the felted room from the cave of the byre.
No window opens of the windows sunk like eyes
In a four-foot wall of stones casually picked
From the knuckly hills on which these houses crawl
Like black and legless beasts who breathe in their sleep

Among the piles of peat and pooks of hay—
A brave oasis in the indifferent moors.
And while the stories circulate like smoke,
The sense of life spreads out from the one-eyed house
In wider circles through the lake of night
In which articulate man has dropped a stone—
In wider circles round the black-faced sheep,
Wider and fainter till they hardly crease
The ebony heritage of the herded dead.
On those islands
The tinkers whom no decent girl will go with,
Preserve the Gaelic tunes unspoiled by contact
With the folk-fancier or the friendly tourist,
And preserve the knowledge of horse-flesh and preserve
The uncompromising empire of the rogue.
On those islands
The tethered cow grazes among the orchises
And figures in blue calico turn by hand
The ground beyond the plough, and the bus, not stopping,
Drops a parcel for the lonely household
Where men remembering stories of eviction
Are glad to have their land though mainly stones—
The honoured bones which still can hoist a body.
On those islands
There is echo of the leaping fish, the identical
Sound that cheered the chiefs at ease from slaughter;
There is echo of baying hounds of a lost breed
And echo of MacCrimmon's pipes lost in the cave;
And seals cry with the voices of the drowned.
When men go out to fish, no one must say 'Good luck'
And the confidences told in a boat at sea
Must be as if printed on the white ribbon of a wave
Withdrawn as soon as printed—so never heard.

On those islands
The black minister paints the tour of hell
While the unregenerate drink from the bottle's neck
In gulps like gauntlets thrown at the devil's head
And spread their traditional songs across the hills
Like fraying tapestries of fights and loves,
The boar-hunt and the rope let down at night—
Lost causes and lingering home-sickness.
On those islands
The fish come singing from the drunken sea,
The herring rush the gunwales and sort themselves
To cram the expectant barrels of their own accord—
Or such is the dream of the fisherman whose wet
Leggings hang on the door as he sleeps returned
From a night when miles of net were drawn up empty.
On those islands
A girl with candid eyes goes out to marry
An independent tenant of seven acres
Who goes each year to the south to work on the roads
In order to raise a rent of forty shillings,
And all the neighbours celebrate their wedding
With drink and pipes and the walls of the barn reflect
The crazy shadows of the whooping dancers.
On those islands
Where many live on the dole or on old-age pensions
And many waste with consumption and some are drowned
And some of the old stumble in the midst of sleep
Into the pot-hole hitherto shunned in dreams
Or falling from the cliff among the shrieks of gulls
Reach the bottom before they have time to wake—
Whoever dies on the islands and however
The whole of the village goes into three-day mourning,
The afflicted home is honoured and the shops are shut

For on those islands
Where a few surnames cover a host of people
And the art of being a stranger with your neighbour
Has still to be imported, death is still
No lottery ticket in a public lottery—
The result to be read on the front page of a journal—
But a family matter near to the whole family.
On those islands
Where no train runs on rails and the tyrant time
Has no clock-towers to signal people to doom
With semaphore ultimatums tick by tick,
There is still peace though not for me and not
Perhaps for long—still peace on the bevel hills
For those who still can live as their fathers lived
On those islands.

1937

It's no go the merrygoround, it's no go the rickshaw,
All we want is a limousine and a ticket for the peepshow.
Their knickers are made of crêpe-de-chine, their shoes
     are made of python,
Their halls are lined with tiger rugs and their walls with
     heads of bison.

John MacDonald found a corpse, put it under the sofa,
Waited till it came to life and hit it with a poker,
Sold its eyes for souvenirs, sold its blood for whiskey,
Kept its bones for dumb-bells to use when he was fifty.

It's no go the Yogi-Man, it's no go Blavatsky,
All we want is a bank balance and a bit of skirt in a taxi.

Annie MacDougall went to milk, caught her foot in
     the heather,
Woke to hear a dance record playing of Old Vienna.
It's no go your maidenheads, it's no go your culture,
All we want is a Dunlop tyre and the devil mend the
     puncture.

The Laird o' Phelps spent Hogmannay declaring he
     was sober;
Counted his feet to prove the fact and found he had
     one foot over.
Mrs. Carmichael had her fifth, looked at the job with
     repulsion,
Said to the midwife "Take it away; I'm through with
     overproduction."

It's no go the gossip column, it's no go the Ceilidh,
All we want is a mother's help and a sugar-stick for the
       baby.

Willie Murray cut his thumb, couldn't count the damage,
Took the hide of an Ayrshire cow and used it for a
       bandage.
His brother caught three hundred cran when the seas were
       lavish,
Threw the bleeders back in the sea and went upon the
       parish.

It's no go the Herring Board, it's no go the Bible,
All we want is a packet of fags when our hands are idle.

It's no go the picture palace, it's no go the stadium,
It's no go the country cot with a pot of pink geraniums.
It's no go the Government grants, it's no go the elections,
Sit on your arse for fifty years and hang your hat on a
       pension.

It's no go my honey love, it's no go my poppet;
Work your hands from day to day, the winds will blow the
       profit.
The glass is falling hour by hour, the glass will fall for ever,
But if you break the bloody glass you won't hold up the
       weather.

1937

NOW THAT THE
SHAPES OF MIST

Now that the shapes of mist like hooded beggar-children
Slink quickly along the middle of the road
And the lamps draw trails of milk in ponds of lustrous lead
I am decidedly pleased not to be dead.

Or when wet roads at night reflect the clutching
Importunate fingers of trees and windy shadows
Lunge and flounce on the windscreen as I drive
I am glad of the accident of being alive.

There are so many nights with stars or close-
ly interleaved with battleship-grey or plum,
So many visitors whose Buddha-like palms are pressed
Against the windowpanes where people take their rest.

Whose favour now is yours to screen your sleep—
You need not hear the strings that are tuning for the
            dawn—
Mingling, my dear, your breath with the quiet breath
Of Sleep whom the old writers called the brother of Death.

                                                1936.

For W. H. Auden

Now the winter nights begin
Lonely comfort walls me in;
So before the memory slip
I review our Iceland trip—

Not for me romantic nor
Idyll on a mythic shore
But a fancy turn, you know,
Sandwiched in a graver show.

Down in Europe Seville fell,
Nations germinating hell,
The Olympic games were run—
Spots upon the Aryan sun.

And the don in me set forth
How the landscape of the north
Had educed the saga style
Plodding forward mile by mile.

And the don in you replied
That the North begins inside,
Our ascetic guts require
Breathers from the Latin fire.

So although no ghost was scotched
We were happy while we watched
Ravens from their walls of shale
Cruise around the rotting whale,

Watched the sulphur basins boil,
Loops of steam uncoil and coil,
While the valley fades away
To a sketch of Judgment Day.

So we rode and joked and smoked
With no miracles evoked,
With no levitations won
In the thin unreal sun;

In that island never found
Visions blossom from the ground,
No conversions like St. Paul,
No great happenings at all.

Holidays should be like this,
Free from over-emphasis,
Time for soul to stretch and spit
Before the world comes back on it,

Before the chimneys row on row
Sneer in smoke, 'We told you so'
And the fog-bound sirens call
Ruin to the long sea-wall.

Rows of books around me stand,
Fence me round on either hand;
Through that forest of dead words
I would hunt the living birds—

Great black birds that fly alone
Slowly through a land of stone,

And the gulls who weave a free
Quilt of rhythm on the sea.

Here in Hampstead I sit late
Nights which no one shares and wait
For the 'phone to ring or for
Unknown angels at the door;

Better were the northern skies
Than this desert in disguise—
Rugs and cushions and the long
Mirror which repeats the song.

For the litany of doubt
From these walls comes breathing out
Till the room becomes a pit
Humming with the fear of it

With the fear of loneliness
And uncommunicableness;
All the wires are cut, my friends
Live beyond the severed ends.

So I write these lines for you
Who have felt the death-wish too,
But your lust for life prevails—
Drinking coffee, telling tales.

Our prerogatives as men
Will be cancelled who knows when;
Still I drink your health before
The gun-butt raps upon the door.

1936